THE LAST LOST FOREST

Written by Peter G. Martin

Illustrated by Faiza Saleem

THE LAST LOST FOREST
Published by Storybook Story Publishing
Santa Barbara, CA USA

Written by Peter G. Martin
Illustrated by Faiza Saleem

Copyright © 2022 by Peter G. Maritn
First Edition, October 2022
Author services by Pedernales Publishing, LLC
www.pedernalespublishing.com
ISBN 978-1-7373053-4-7 Hardcover Edition
ISBN 978-1-7373053-5-4 Paperback Edition
ISBN 978-1-7373053-3-0 Digital Edition
Library of Congress Control Number: 2022914467
Printed in the United States of America

Written by Peter G. Martin
Illustrated by Faiza Saleem

Once upon a time there lived a brother and sister called Avi and Anna. They loved to play together in the backyard, snack on jellybeans, and dream about going on fantastical adventures.

One day, Avi and Anna chased each other into a huge spiderweb in the corner of the backyard. They expected to be covered in webs, but they were surprised to see what happened next.

Suddenly, everything was dark, and they tumbled through
a long, dark passageway. Anna cried out, "Help me, Avi!"
Avi shouted to Anna, "Hold my hand, and we will be safe together."

The children landed with a loud WHOMP, and they both shrieked, "Ow, Ow, Ow!" They looked around and found themselves in a room of a house in the middle of a huge, dark forest.

Anna and Avi ran to look out of the windows and were amazed to see nothing but trees in every direction. Anna said, "Where are we?" "I don't know," replied Avi.

After a while, Anna and Avi decided to go outside and explore the forest. As they opened the door, they saw that the trees were all gigantic and made them feel very small.

They headed away from the house and found a large path. Anna and Avi pulled out some jellybeans they had in their pockets and decided to drop them on the ground so that they could find their way back to the house. As they continued walking, they came to a fork in the path. They turned to the right.

As they kept on walking, the path began to get smaller and smaller and brought more twists and turns. As they looked around them, they started to see big, bright eyes looking at them through the forest. "It feels like the trees are watching us," said Avi.

The further they walked, the path began to get narrower,
the trees got bigger and the eyes watching them became brighter.
They also started to hear weird whooping and whooshing
noises coming from behind the trees.

It began to get darker and darker, and Anna and Avi grew more and more afraid. "Let's go back to the house, I'm scared," said Anna. So, they decided to turn around.

Anna and Avi began walking faster and faster, following the jellybean trail that they had left. However, when they came to the fork in the path, they saw that all the jellybeans had disappeared.

Anna and Avi could not decide which way to go. They looked
down one path and then the other and began to cry.
"I don't know which path we should take," cried Avi.

Then Anna decided that they should split up, so that one of them might find the trail of jellybeans that led back to the house. Avi said, "Are you sure we should split up? It can be very scary by yourself," but Anna nodded her head.

They both walked down each path very slowly, looking around at the forest. With each step they took, they became more and more afraid.

Suddenly Avi let out a huge scream, and
Anna ran back quickly to see what was happening.
Anna shouted, "Avi, what's the matter?"

When Anna turned the corner, she saw a huge monster with 3 heads, 5 legs, and 2 arms standing between her and Avi. Anna said, "Don't worry, Avi, I have a plan!"

Anna told Avi not to be afraid and asked him to sing
a high-pitched song to distract the monster. So Avi began
to sing, "La, La, La, La." Anna said, "Great job, Avi, it's working!"

The monster became hypnotized by the beautiful notes Avi sang. Anna then started to sing the same high-pitched song, "La, La, La, La," from behind the monster, who was now surrounded by sound.

Suddenly the monster fell into a trance and crashed to the ground.
As Avi ran past the monster to get back to Anna, he saw a glint of
light from the back of one of the monster's heads. Avi said,
"Lets search the monster for treasure!"

They found a shiny silver key tucked
behind one of the monster's necks. And Avi said,
"What shall we do with the monster?" Anna replied,
"Let's leave it to recover, so it can go back to its family."

Look! A key!

Avi held up the key, and it suddenly began to glow.
He pointed it down the left path and it glowed even brighter.
The key was telling them where to go!

Anna and Avi followed the glowing key all
the way back to the house, where they realized
that the key might help them get back home.

They decided to search the house for a place
the key might fit. But nothing they tried worked.
Then Anna remembered that, when they had arrived
in the house, they had landed on the kitchen floor.

They went into the kitchen, pulled up the rug, and found a locked trap door. Avi put the key into the lock, and it opened immediately.

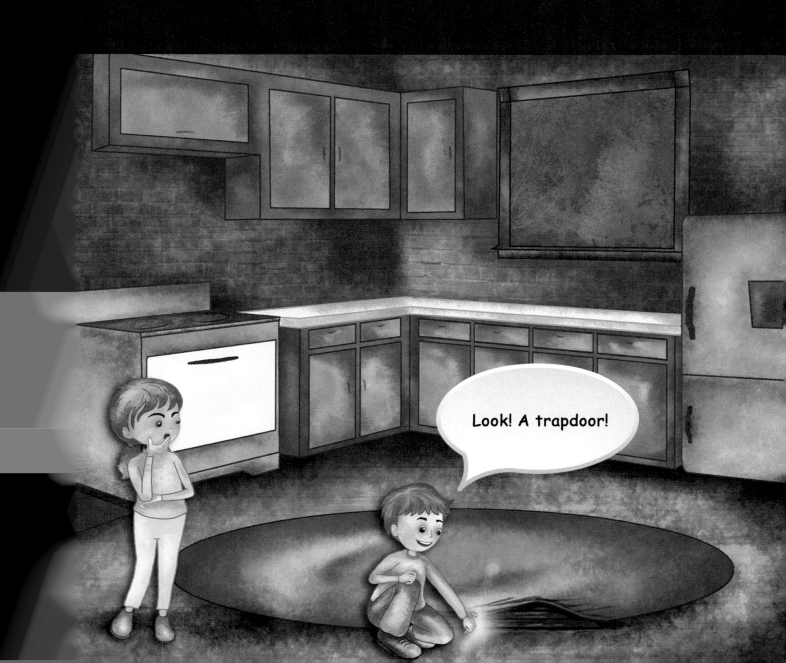

and saw a huge spiderweb in the middle of the magical room.
"I hope this takes us back home!" yelled Avi.
They held hands, closed their eyes, and ran toward the spiderweb.

Suddenly, the children were enveloped in darkness again.
They found themselves tumbling through a long, dark passageway,
but this time they were not scared.

Anna and Avi landed with a WHOMP, but this time they
fell onto something soft. They opened their eyes to see that
they had landed on the grass in the backyard of their own house.
Avi smiled and said, "We made it!" They were so happy to be home.

Avi looked at the spiderweb in the corner of the backyard and asked Anna, "Shall we close the portal to the last lost forest?" Anna smiled at Avi and said, "No, let's leave it open for other children to find, so they can have fantastical adventures of their own. It will be our little secret," she smiled.

Dear reader,

Your purchase helps to provide kind and loving support to those touched by pediatric cancer. We are proudly donating a percentage of the proceeds from the sale of each book to support the families and children served by the Teddy Bear Cancer Foundation – often by providing the immediate out of pocket, non–medical expenditures that are rarely reimbursable.

Mission Statement: Empowering families living in Santa Barbara, Ventura and San Luis Obispo counties that have a child with cancer by providing financial, educational and emotional support.

Made in the USA
Las Vegas, NV
05 June 2025

23177979R00021